DATE DUE			

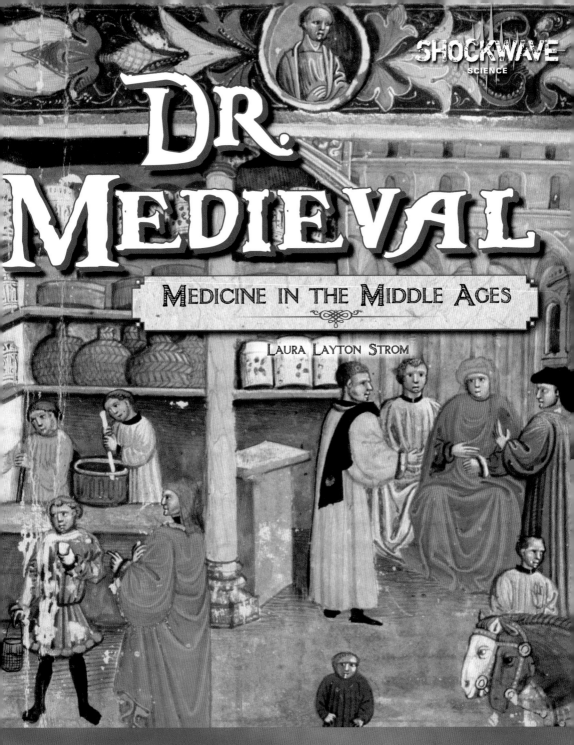

SHOCKWAVE
SCIENCE

DR. MEDIEVAL

MEDICINE IN THE MIDDLE AGES

LAURA LAYTON STROM

children's press®

An imprint of Scholastic Inc.

NEW YORK • TORONTO • LONDON • AUCKLAND • SYDNEY
MEXICO CITY • NEW DELHI • HONG KONG
DANBURY, CONNECTICUT

610
STR
C.I
2008
11.16

Library of Congress Cataloging-in-Publication Data

Strom, Laura Layton.
  Dr. Medieval : medicine in the Middle Ages / by Laura Layton Strom.
      p. cm. -- (Shockwave)
  Includes index.
  ISBN-10: 0-531-17765-3 (lib. bdg.)
  ISBN-13: 978-0-531-17765-5 (lib. bdg.)
  ISBN-10: 0-531-18797-7 (pbk.)
  ISBN-13: 978-0-531-18797-5 (pbk.)

  1. Medicine, Medieval--History--Juvenile literature. I. Title.
  II. Series.

  R141.S77 2008
  610--dc22

2007016472

Published in 2008 by Children's Press, an imprint of Scholastic Inc.,
557 Broadway, New York, New York 10012
www.scholastic.com

08 09 10 11 12 13 14 15 16 17
10 9 8 7 6 5 4 3 2 1

Printed in China through Colorcraft Ltd., Hong Kong

Author: Laura Layton Strom
Educational Consultant: Ian Morrison
Editor: Karen Alexander
Designer: Avon Willis
Photo Researcher: Jamshed Mistry
Illustrations: Jeannie Ferguson (Dr Medieval, cover; p. 8; p. 12; pp. 22–23; pp. 28–29);
Helen Bacon (medieval cure quizz, p. 29)

Photographs by: Avon Willis (comfrey, feverfew, sage, thyme, p. 16); **Big Stock Photo** (leech,
blood spots, p. 3; spider, p. 13; leech, blood spots, pp. 14–15; rosemary, p. 16; scientist,
pp. 30–31); **Getty Images** (contemporary scientist, p. 13; p. 28); **Jamshed Mistry** (lavender,
p. 16); **Jennifer and Brian Lupton** (teenagers, pp. 30–31); **Photolibrary** (p. 1; p. 5; p. 7;
surgery, p. 9; p. 10; Galen, p. 11; urea, p. 13; patient with leeches, p. 15; gathering dill,
p. 17; p. 19; King Kalman, woman being ducked, p. 21; town crier, burial, pp. 24–25;
pp. 26–27); **Prisma/Ancient Art & Architecture Ltd.** (preparing vinegar mixture, p. 17);
StockXpert.com (pot, p. 23); **©Topfoto/www.stockcentral.co.nz** (Hippocrates, p. 11; p. 18);
Tranz/Corbis (background town, cover; university scholars, p. 9; checking pulse, p. 13;
p. 14; p. 20; Matthew Hopkins, p. 21; Carcassonne, p. 23; plague victim, p. 24; flea, p. 25)

All illustrations and other photographs © Weldon Owen Education Inc.

CONTENTS

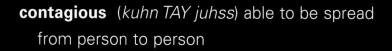

contagious (*kuhn TAY juhss*) able to be spread from person to person

diagnose (*dye ugh NOHSS*) to decide what illness a person has

Hippocratic (*hi puh KRA tik*) **oath** a promise still made by many doctors, to work for the best health of their patients

Middle Ages the period of European history from about 500 A.D. to about 1500 A.D.

physician (*fuh ZISH uhn*) a medical doctor ——————

plague (*PLAYG*) a very contagious disease caused by bacteria

superstition (*soo pur STIH shuhn*) a belief in things that cannot be explained or proved

vaccinate (*VAK suh nate*) to give someone a medicine that prepares the body to fight a particular disease

· ·

For easy reference, see Wordmark on back flap.
For additional vocabulary, see Glossary on page 32.

Although the word *contagious* is usually associated with disease, it is also used when describing someone's attitude; both a smile and anger can be contagious.

5

The Romans, from Italy, ruled most of western Europe for 800 years. Their power ended when their empire was overthrown by wandering tribes in 476 A.D. The next 1,000 years, until about 1500 A.D., were called the **Middle Ages**.

During the Middle Ages, many people still spoke Latin – the language that was spoken during the time of the Roman Empire. *Medieval* is from the Latin words for the "Middle Ages." Life was hard in medieval times. Many people died when they were quite young. If people survived all the childhood illnesses, they might live to be forty or fifty years old. Thirty was considered old!

Much of the knowledge that had been gained since ancient times was lost to Europeans when the Roman Empire ended. **Superstition** and religious beliefs were important parts of medieval life. People often believed that illness was caused by evil spirits. It wasn't until the **Renaissance** that medical knowledge really began to advance.

Curious Cures

Medieval cures usually didn't work. Often they even made the problem worse!

PROBLEM:	Plague	Battle wound	Fever	Swollen neck glands
MEDIEVAL CURE:	Lay a dried toad or a live hen on the lumps to draw out the poison.	Pour boiling oil over it.	You obviously have too much blood – let some out.	Touch the king or queen, or a coin that the king or queen has touched.

A dying man tells his will to a writer while a doctor checks him and a **monk** prays for him. Medieval medicine was a combination of science and superstition.

Snakebite	Toothache	Madness	Leprosy or blindness
Put earwax on the bite and ask a priest to pray for you.	Go to a tooth-puller at a fair. Get some drummers to play so that people won't hear your cries of pain.	Get a surgeon to cut open the skull and take out the stones that are making you insane.	Go to Canterbury Cathedral in England and pray to Saint Thomas à Becket.

I INTRODUCE MYSELF

 am Dr. Medieval. I am keeping this journal so that those who come after me will know what it was like to be a **physician** in these times.

When I was fourteen, I went to study at a **monastery**. The monastery library had many ancient Greek and Roman writings. I was able to study the writings of the ancient physicians Hippocrates (*hi PAH kruh teez*) and Galen (*GAY luhn*). I was inspired to become a physician too.

The head of the monastery is an **enlightened** man. He sent me to the University of Paris to train. It took me seven years. I believe in learning, not superstition. I believe in studying my patients carefully – and I have plenty of them to study!

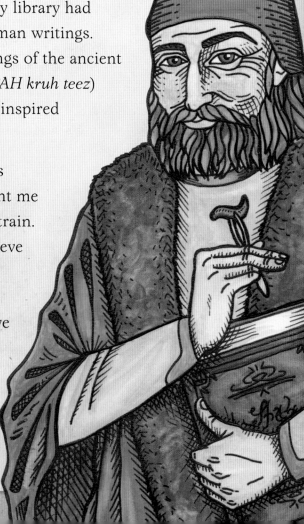

In medieval times, very few physicians were trained. Most medieval people believed in lucky charms, such as four-leaf clovers. They believed in special prayers and chants, or strange rituals, to cure illnesses.

◀ **Scholars at the University of Paris in the Middle Ages**

▼ Doctors learn about how the human body works by **dissecting** dead bodies. Here Guy de Chauliac, a famous fourteenth-century surgeon, gives a dissection lesson at the University of Montpellier, France.

A Matter of Humors

Hippocrates and Galen said that everything in the world comes from four elements: water, earth, air, and fire. They believed that each element controls one of the four humors, or liquids, in the body. The humors are **phlegm** (*FLEM),* controlled by water; black bile, controlled by earth; blood, controlled by air; and **yellow bile**, controlled by fire. The physicians believed that the humors give people their **temperaments**. They said that people become ill when their bodies have too much or too little of these humors. The seasons, the weather, and the planets affect the humors.

THE FOUR TEMPERAMENTS

PHLEGMATIC

Phlegmatic people are calm and sensitive. However, too much phlegm can make people moody and lazy.

MELANCHOLIC

Melancholic (*mel uhn KAH lik*) people are calm and creative. However, too much black bile can make people sad.

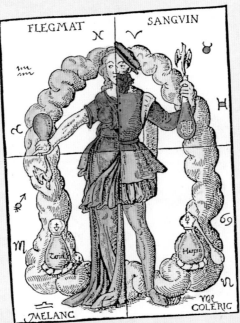

SANGUINE

Sanguine (*SAN gwin*) people are brave and cheerful. However, too much blood can make people act without thinking.

CHOLERIC

Choleric (*KAH luh rik*) people have plenty of energy. However, too much yellow bile can cause people to get angry quickly.

10

Hippocrates

HIPPOCRATES

Hippocrates was born in Greece in about 460 B.C. At the time, people believed that illness had supernatural causes. Hippocrates said that illness had physical causes. He believed in natural cures. Hippocrates is thought to have written the **Hippocratic oath** – a set of rules for physicians. Many doctors still take the oath. Hippocrates didn't become famous until hundreds of years after he died. He may not actually have said all that we think he said. However, he is still considered to be the father of medicine.

Galen learned how to heal sick and injured people by treating gladiators.

GALEN

Galen was born at Pergamum, in present-day Turkey, about 130 A.D. He became the physician to the city's **gladiators**. Later, Galen moved to Rome, where he became physician to several Roman emperors. Galen believed that physicians needed to learn about the workings of the human body by dissecting bodies. It was he who realized that arteries carry blood. Until then, it was believed that they carried air. Galen's writings influenced medicine for the next 1,400 years.

And So to Work

Winter 1346 A.D.

 usually visit my patients in their homes. In my physician's bag, I carry the herbs that I use to make medicines.

I find it important to check my patient's humors. I take my patient's pulse to check the strength of the heartbeat. However, the most important medical tool that I carry is my urine chart. I study the color of my patient's urine. Sometimes I taste it too! From the urine's color, I can determine what illness the patient has. If there is blood in the urine, then death is surely on the way.

Guess the Medieval Cure!

The patient has chills, a headache, a fever, and spots all over her body. It could be smallpox. What do you think a medieval doctor might have done?

A. sprinkled perfume around the room

B. fed the patient chicken soup

C. surrounded the patient with red cloth

Answer on page 29

It looks as if these journal entries might continue on the even-numbered pages and use the same background color. That will really help me separate the journal from the rest.

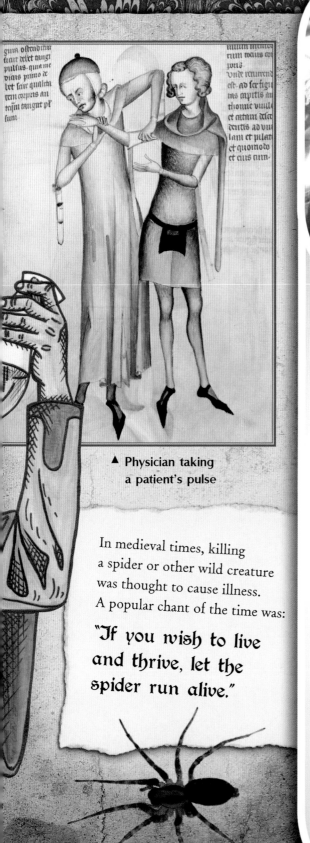

▲ Physician taking a patient's pulse

In medieval times, killing a spider or other wild creature was thought to cause illness. A popular chant of the time was:

"If you wish to live and thrive, let the spider run alive."

TRUTH!

Urine is still used to help **diagnose** some diseases, such as cancer and diabetes, and to check health. However, urine color is not an accurate way to determine an illness. Many things can affect the color of urine. Blackberries and beets can turn it pink or red. Also, blood in the urine doesn't always mean certain death! It may be caused by an infection or even by strenuous exercise. It is usually treatable.

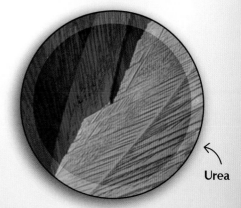

← Urea

Urea is one of the body's main waste products. It is flushed from the body in the urine. The photograph shows urea magnified 100 times.

IT'S ALL IN THE BLOOD

Spring 1347 A.D.

M y patients' blood can tell me many things about their health. Sometimes I taste their blood. I believe that the blood of a sick person is bitter or sour. One of the cures that I use frequently is bloodletting. I use a **lancet** to cut open a vein and let the bad blood flow out.

My leeches are a precious remedy. I always carry them with me. I gather them from a pond near the monastery. If a patient has a headache, I attach several leeches to the forehead so they can suck the blood and relieve the pain. If my patient has an earache, I attach a leech to the earlobe.

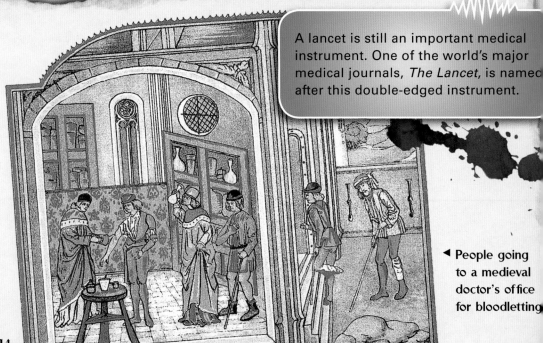

A lancet is still an important medical instrument. One of the world's major medical journals, *The Lancet*, is named after this double-edged instrument.

◀ People going to a medieval doctor's office for bloodletting

Physicians treating an illness with leeches

TRUTH!

Bloodletting was used as a cure for almost anything in the Middle Ages, and for hundreds of years afterward. Severe blood loss may have killed many people. There is no such thing as bad blood. Nor is there such a thing as too much blood.

Leeches were used so much in medieval medicine that *leech* was another word for *doctor*. Today, leeches are again being used in medicine. When leeches bite, they inject the victim with an **antibiotic**, an **anticoagulant**, and a substance that widens the blood vessels. This allows blood to flow more easily. These substances help patients to recover after surgery.

SHOCKER

Bloodletting may have contributed to the death of the first U.S. president, George Washington, in 1799. He was bled four times on the day of his death, losing about five pints of blood. Washington was being treated for a sore throat!

Leech

15

HERBS FOR HEALING

Summer 1347 A.D.

The medications that I use are made mostly from herbs. Brother Richard has taught me that God provides cures in nature for many human ills. The monastery has a large **infirmary garden**. I gather my herbs there. I also go out into the countryside to gather the herbs that the wise woman Martha has told me of.

Lavender eases headaches, relieves tension, and helps people sleep.

Feverfew relieves headaches, insect bites, and breathing problems.

Thyme helps colds and indigestion. A **poultice** can reduce swelling.

Comfrey is also called "knitbone." It aids chest infections. The leaves make a good poultice for sprains, burns, and boils.

Rosemary eases back pain and prevents baldness.

Sage soothes sore throats and aids liver disorders.

I like the way the "Truth!" section appears on the odd-numbered pages. I look forward to reading the truth about the beliefs from long ago. I can sometimes predict what will be in these sections.

TRUTH!

Herbs have been used as remedies throughout history. They are still popular with many people, although there is disagreement about whether they are effective. Although some bacteria and fungi are natural antibiotics, many sick people died in medieval times because there were no medicines that killed the bacteria that caused some illnesses. It was not until the 1940s that drug companies began to develop antibiotics commercially.

▲ The two people at the table are preparing a pepper-and-vinegar mixture for digestion problems.

Medieval Cure for Stomachache

Eat food soaked and cooked in olive oil, fish juice, and salt every morning. Do not eat bread. Drink spinach juice or cabbage juice.

▲ A woman and her daughter gather dill, which was used to ease stomach upsets.

OUR HOSPITAL

The monastery in our town is known for the care it gives to the sick and the dying. On most days, I stop by the hospital to help. The hospital is under the care of Brother Richard, who is a gifted healer.

Brother Richard thinks that lack of cleanliness helps spread disease. We try to keep the hospital clean, but it is not easy. The people who come here are very poor. They are unwashed and smelly. Many of them are dressed in filthy rags. They are covered with lice and fleas.

Recently, we have seen more patients with leprosy. This terrible disease eats away at the skin and bones. The rotting flesh smells terrible. It is a very **contagious** disease. People with leprosy are not allowed to live near other people. We have been given a shelter out of town where these poor outcasts can live. The monks will give them food.

▲ In medieval times, most hospitals were run by monks and nuns.

SHOCKER

People used to believe that lepers got leprosy as a punishment for their sins. King Philip IV of France wanted to burn all the lepers in his kingdom, but the church stopped him.

▲ Lepers went from house to house begging for food. They had to ring bells or shake wooden paddles called clappers to warn people they were coming. That way, people could keep away from them.

Guess the Medieval Cure!

The patient has signs of leprosy: sores, rotting fingers, and weak muscles.

What might the doctor have done?

A. sent the patient to a priest to be declared legally dead
B. cut off the patient's fingers
C. put milk on the patient's sores

Answer on page 29

Leprosy

Assumption	Truth
• very contagious	• somewhat contagious
• people with it must be isolated	• people don't need to be isolated
• caused by sin	• caused by bacteria

TRUTH!

Leprosy is caused by bacteria. Even today, about six million people in the world have the disease. Although there is no cure, leprosy is not usually fatal. Nor is it as contagious as was once thought. People exposed to leprosy rarely catch it. Once people have been exposed to it, they develop an immunity to it. In addition, people with leprosy can take special drugs that prevent the disease from getting worse. These drugs also make the leprosy noncontagious.

WITCH HUNT

oday is a sad day for me. The wise woman Martha has been accused of being a witch! Soldiers came and took her away. Martha is known for her great skill with herbs. She and Brother Richard taught me nearly everything I know about remedies.

Last week, Martha was called to the castle to treat the lord, who had taken ill. After three days, the lord recovered. That miserable castle doctor is jealous of Martha's skills, so he called her a witch. The priest at the castle supports him.

Brother Richard and I are riding over to see if we can help Martha. The beliefs and fears of some people make being a healer a very dangerous business!

▲ In medieval times, people accused of being witches were often burned to death.

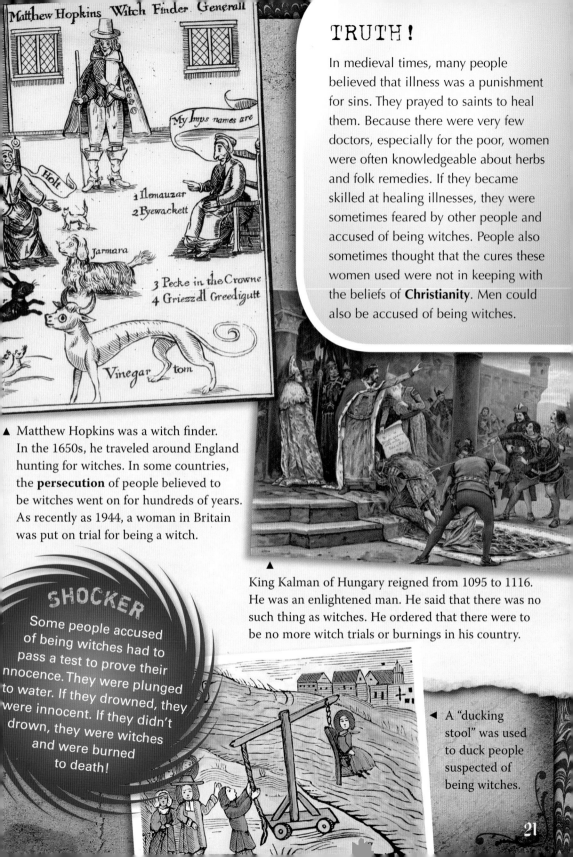

Matthew Hopkins Witch Finder Generall

My Imps names are

Holt

1 Ilemauzar
2 Pyewackett

Jarmara

3 Pecke in the Crowne
4 Griezzell Greediguth

Vinegar tom

TRUTH!

In medieval times, many people believed that illness was a punishment for sins. They prayed to saints to heal them. Because there were very few doctors, especially for the poor, women were often knowledgeable about herbs and folk remedies. If they became skilled at healing illnesses, they were sometimes feared by other people and accused of being witches. People also sometimes thought that the cures these women used were not in keeping with the beliefs of **Christianity**. Men could also be accused of being witches.

▲ Matthew Hopkins was a witch finder. In the 1650s, he traveled around England hunting for witches. In some countries, the **persecution** of people believed to be witches went on for hundreds of years. As recently as 1944, a woman in Britain was put on trial for being a witch.

SHOCKER

Some people accused of being witches had to pass a test to prove their innocence. They were plunged into water. If they drowned, they were innocent. If they didn't drown, they were witches and were burned to death!

▲ King Kalman of Hungary reigned from 1095 to 1116. He was an enlightened man. He said that there was no such thing as witches. He ordered that there were to be no more witch trials or burnings in his country.

◄ A "ducking stool" was used to duck people suspected of being witches.

DIRT AND DESPAIR

Spring 1348 A.D.

oday, I turn thirty. I feel like the old man I am. I have seen too much sickness. Too many babies and children die. I wish I had more knowledge so that I could do more to help them.

Our town is growing too quickly. People come here fleeing from disease elsewhere. **Serfs** come here hoping for freedom. If they can live in a town for a year and a day, they become **freemen**. The increase in population means there is less work. People are starving. There are beggars everywhere.

The streets are filthy. Trash, even human waste, is flung from the windows. The smell is terrible. The dirt and the overcrowding are bad for people's health. There are rats everywhere. I fear **plague** will come to us again in the summer.

Guess the Medieval Cure!

This patient has black and blue blotches all over her body. What might the doctor have done?

A. spread egg whites all over the patient
B. given the patient herb treacle
C. wrapped the patient in bandages and shaved her hair

Answer on page 29

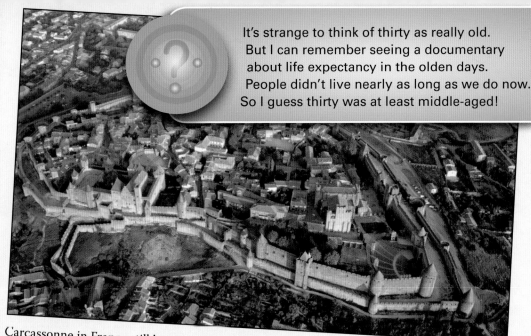

It's strange to think of thirty as really old. But I can remember seeing a documentary about life expectancy in the olden days. People didn't live nearly as long as we do now. So I guess thirty was at least middle-aged!

Carcassonne in France still has its medieval walls. Today, though, most of the city lies outside the walls. During the Middle Ages, most cities and large towns had walls with gates. The gates were often closed at night for safety. They could also be closed to keep sick people out.

TRUTH!

Very few toilets existed in medieval times. Most people used a jar, like the one below, or a bowl. When it was full, the contents were tipped into the streets. Diseases such as typhoid, cholera, and smallpox were common in cities. Rich people often left the cities in summer and went to their country homes where it was healthier because it was less crowded.

Bring Out Your Dead

Summer 1348 A.D.

 hat I feared has come to pass. Plague is upon us. Hundreds of people are dying every day. The very air is full of the smell of death.

We are doing the best we can at the hospital. I have tried using leeches to suck the bad blood out of plague victims. But no matter what I do, the skin turns purplish black and death soon follows. In truth, all we can really do is comfort the dying.

Some people say that plague is a punishment from God. They say the world will soon come to an end. I do not believe that; nor does Brother Richard. We think it is caused by the filth in our towns. There is no way to escape plague. It is in the water, which people draw from unclean wells. It is in the very air!

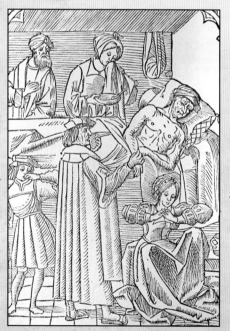

◄ Doctors could not help plague victims. Those who tried often ended up catching the disease themselves.

So many people died of plague ► that there were not enough coffins. Bodies were buried together in pits.

People warm themselves at a fire as a cart collects the bodies of plague victims. Families put their dead in the street to be collected. A crier went ahead of the cart, ringing a bell and calling, "Bring out your dead!" Houses in which there were sick people had a cross and the words, "Lord have mercy on this house" painted on the door. It was both a prayer and a warning to the healthy to stay away. ▼

TRUTH!

Between 1347 and 1353, more than 30 million people in Europe died from plague. That was a third of the entire population. It was not until 1894 that Swiss scientist Alexandre Yersin found that the disease was caused by bacteria that infected rats and rat fleas. The disease was passed on to people when they were bitten by the fleas, or when they breathed in droplets of moisture coughed up by infected people. Victims developed a high fever and a terrible headache. Plague could kill its victims very quickly. Plague still occurs today, but the availability of antibiotics means it need no longer be deadly.

Plague

Plague infection can be seen projecting like a dark finger into the blood-filled stomach of a rat flea.

No cure in the 1300s

Spread by fleas

Killed 30 million people

Plague

Could kill very quickly

High fever and terrible headache

The End of the World?

In 1350, the Italian writer Petrarch wrote to a friend: "There was a crowd of us; now we are almost alone. We should make new friends, but how, when the human race is almost wiped out; and why, when it looks to me as if the end of the world is at hand?"

HOPES FOR HEALTH

Fall 1348 A.D.

Brother Richard and I escaped plague. Many of those we knew were not so lucky. With Brother Richard's skills as an herbalist and my skills as a physician, we hope to improve the health of the townspeople. We have asked Matthew, the barber-surgeon, to help us in our work.

When I visited London, I saw that water is passed from rivers through **conduits** to tanks. We hope to pipe water from a spring that lies above the town, so that people can get clean water.

Rotten teeth cause deep distress to many people. Some of my patients have died from poison in their blood caused by bad teeth. My bloodletting failed to help them. I have noticed that the rich, who eat meat, honey, and white bread, have worse teeth than the peasants. The peasants eat coarse bread, vegetables, and fruit. I tell my patients to chew twigs or rub their teeth with salt to clean them.

◄ A dentist uses a rope to pull out a tooth. Chewing on black peppercorns or cloves was thought to help the pain. People still use cloves to ease toothache.

**Surgical tools used ►
in the Middle Ages**

Dr. Medieval was right about diet. Plenty of vegetables, fruit, and whole grains help to keep us healthy. In medieval times, tooth decay was a big problem. Many people had lost all their teeth by the time they were sixteen. Early toothbrushes were made from coarse hair, such as pig bristles.

SHOCKER

People believed that toothache was caused by worms gnawing at the teeth. One cure was to burn a candle inside the mouth. The worms would then fall out.

For thousands of years, trepanning was used to cure brain diseases. Archaeologists have found 8,000-year-old skulls with holes drilled in them. A hole was cut in the patient's head to let out the evil spirits that were causing the pain. Trepanning is used now only in rare kinds of surgery.

In the Middle Ages, there was no **anesthetic**. Limbs were cut off only if the person would die otherwise. Many patients died anyway – from shock, blood loss, or infection.

A Shave or an Operation?

Surgeons were not considered to be as skilled as physicians. The early surgeons were barbers. The traditional red-and-white-striped barber's pole represents the blood and the bandages. In fact, the first official British organization for surgeons was called the College of Barber Surgeons.

CELEBRATION TIME

Summer 1349 A.D.

Today, there was a great celebration in our town. Young Lady Beatrice at the castle is to be married. It was also a celebration for me. The castle doctor has been exposed as a **charlatan**. I have been asked to replace him. I shall be able to spread my ideas about health and hygiene more widely.

I went to the **tournament** being staged in honor of Beatrice. The jousting was exciting to watch. Everyone had a favorite knight to cheer for. Lady Beatrice gave her scarf to a handsome knight in blue-and-silver armor. My services were not much required. No one was badly hurt. One knight injured his arm, but I soon had the broken lance out and the wound cleaned and bound.

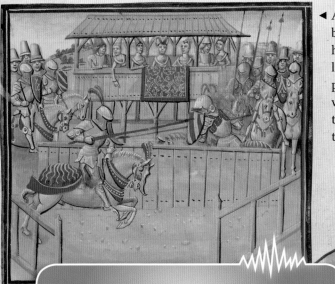

◀ A joust was a mock fight between two knights on horses. They each had a lance – a long rod with a pointed steel tip. Jousting was a way for knights to practice their skills.

It is believed the word *charlatan* comes from the Italian *ciarlatano*, which means "a person who travels from place to place selling useless medicines."

Page 12:
The correct answer is C.
Hanging colored cloths around
the patient was a common treatment
for smallpox in medieval times.

Page 19:
The correct answer is A.
During medieval times,
priests performed a
special ritual in which
the leper was separated
from the community
and declared to be
legally dead.

Page 22:
The correct answer is B.
Herb treacle was a medieval treatment
to cure anything from fever to plague.
More than 60 ingredients went into
the treacle, including roasted skins
of snakes! If the patient recovered,
it was good
fortune, not
good medicine.

29

Medieval doctors often couldn't cure even minor illnesses. They didn't have antibiotics or any of the other medicines available now. Today, doctors can cure all kinds of diseases. They can even **vaccinate** people to prevent them from getting the diseases in the first place. Widespread vaccination programs mean that some diseases, such as smallpox, have been almost wiped out.

WHAT DO YOU THINK?

Do you believe children should have to be vaccinated for some diseases before they are allowed to go to school?

PRO

We are lucky we are alive today and able to benefit from medical advances such as vaccines. If we had lived 1,000 years ago, many of us would have died as babies. If vaccinations can wipe out serious diseases, then I think they should be compulsory.

In most of the United States, children must be vaccinated against a number of diseases, such as diphtheria and polio, before they can go to school. Some people argue that people should not be required by law to have vaccinations. That is because some people believe vaccination is wrong – either because they oppose it for religious reasons, or because they believe vaccinations can cause health problems.

CON

It's great that scientists can develop medicines that cure diseases. However, people's rights are important too. If parents believe vaccination is wrong, or there are risks involved, then they have the right to choose whether their children are vaccinated.

Go to **www.learner.org/ exhibits/middleages/ morhealt.html** to learn more about medieval medicine.